Lerner SPORTS

ALL-STAR SMACKDOWN

SAUCE GARDNER VS. DEION SANDERS

WHO WOULD WIN?

YOLANDA RIDGE

Lerner Publications ◆ Minneapolis

Copyright © 2025 by Lerner Publishing Group, Inc.

All rights reserved. International copyright secured. No part of this book may be reproduced, stored in a retrieval system, or transmitted in any form or by any means—electronic, mechanical, photocopying, recording, or otherwise—without the prior written permission of Lerner Publishing Group, Inc., except for the inclusion of brief quotations in an acknowledged review.

Lerner Publications Company
An imprint of Lerner Publishing Group, Inc.
241 First Avenue North
Minneapolis, MN 55401 USA

For reading levels and more information, look up this title at www.lernerbooks.com.

Main body text set in Aptifer Sans LT Pro.
Typeface provided by Linotype AG.

Editor: Nicole Berglund **Photo Editor:** Nicole Berglund

Library of Congress Cataloging-in-Publication Data
Names: Ridge, Yolanda, 1973– author.
Title: Sauce Gardner vs. Deion Sanders : who would win? / Yolanda Ridge.
Description: Minneapolis, MN : Lerner Publications, [2025] | Series: All-star smackdown (Lerner sports) | Includes bibliographical references and index. | Audience: Ages 7–11 | Audience: Grades 2–3 | Summary: "Sauce Gardner and Deion Sanders both rose to fame as NFL cornerbacks. But who is the true king of the defensive back? Compare their careers side by side, then choose a winner!"— Provided by publisher.
Identifiers: LCCN 2024006412 (print) | LCCN 2024006413 (ebook) | ISBN 9798765648261 (library binding) | ISBN 9798765653234 (epub)
Subjects: LCSH: Football—United States—Juvenile literature. | Football players—Rating of—Juvenile literature. | Sanders, Deion,—Juvenile literature. | Gardner, Ahmad, 2000-—Juvenile literature. | Cornerbacks (Football)—United States—Biography—Juvenile literature.
Classification: LCC GV950.7 .R53 2025 (print) | LCC GV950.7 (ebook) | DDC 796.332—dc23/eng/20240213

LC record available at https://lccn.loc.gov/2024006412
LC ebook record available at https://lccn.loc.gov/2024006413

Manufactured in the United States of America
1-1010829-53384-4/11/2024

TABLE OF CONTENTS

Introduction
Changing the Game 4

Chapter 1
Speeding to Victory 8

Chapter 2
Going Pro 14

Chapter 3
Building a Champion 20

Chapter 4
And the Winner Is 24

Smackdown Breakdown 28
Glossary 30
Learn More 31
Index 32

Sauce Gardner

INTRODUCTION
CHANGING THE GAME

New York Jets cornerback Sauce Gardner was off to a fiery rookie season. In November 2022, his team took on the Buffalo Bills. The Jets were down by four points in the second half.

 Fast Facts

- Deion Sanders was an eight-time Pro Bowl player.
- Sanders won the Super Bowl two years in a row with two different teams.
- Sauce Gardner won the National Football League (NFL) Defensive Rookie of the Year in 2022.
- Gardner was one of the few rookie cornerbacks to become a first-team All-Pro player.

Bills quarterback Josh Allen threw the ball. Gardner intercepted the throw and ran for the end zone. Touchdown! The Jets were now ahead by three, but Gardner wasn't done.

With 33 seconds left in the game, Allen threw a long pass. If caught, the Bills would have the lead again and probably the win. Gardner ran at full speed. Then he reached up. He knocked the ball away from the wide receiver. The Jets won 20–17.

Gardner's play turned everything around for the Jets. He had only played nine games in the NFL. Yet he was already proving himself a valuable player on his team.

Deion Sanders

Deion Sanders made great plays early in his career too. In the first game of his rookie season in 1989, Sanders caught a punt. Then he ran over half the length of the football field to the end zone. Touchdown!

Sanders and Gardner are both cornerbacks. They stick close to wide receivers and make it hard for them to catch the ball. Quarterbacks don't often throw the ball to receivers who are closely guarded by cornerbacks. But if they do throw it, cornerbacks can intercept it. Or they can knock it away in a pass breakup.

Cornerbacks make exciting plays. Learn more about their game-changing moments. Then decide which cornerback you think is best!

Gardner greets fans before a game in 2022.

Sanders, playing for the Dallas Cowboys, runs with the ball during a 1997 game.

CHAPTER 1

Gardner, playing for the University of Cincinnati Bearcats, keeps his eyes on the ball during a 2021 game.

SPEEDING TO VICTORY

Sauce Gardner focused on football at his high school in Detroit, Michigan. He used his speed to play both cornerback and wide receiver. Before entering his senior year, Gardner was named a top 30 player in his home state.

In 2019, Gardner was a game changer in his first year at the University of Cincinnati. That season, the Bearcats won the American Athletic Conference East Division and the Birmingham Bowl.

Gardner made the College Football All-America Team his junior year. He was also the conference Defensive Player of the Year. He entered the NFL Draft in 2022 after he graduated. The New York Jets chose him with the fourth overall pick.

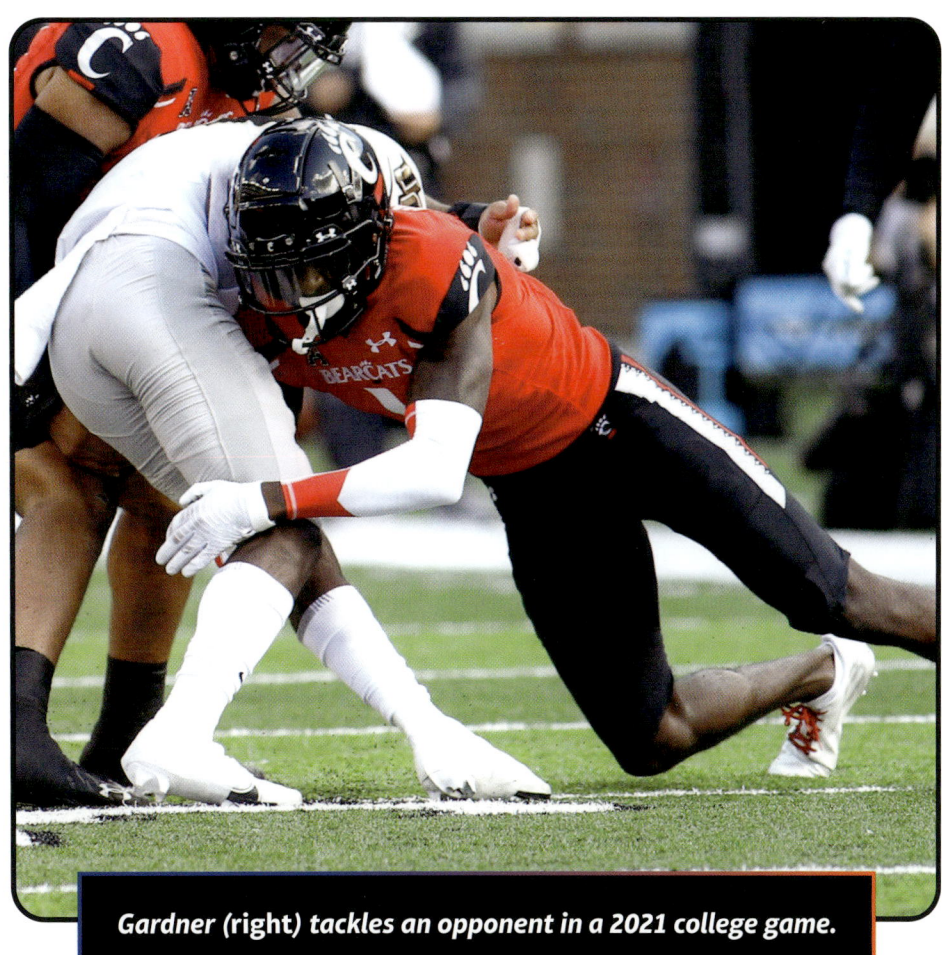

Gardner (right) tackles an opponent in a 2021 college game.

Gardner (right) focuses during a college game in 2021.

CONSIDER THIS
Sauce Gardner's real first name is Ahmad. The nickname Sauce came from one of his former football coaches. Deion Sanders earned his nickname Prime Time in high school. A friend gave him the name after his amazing performance in a basketball game.

Deion Sanders has always been an athlete. He played many sports growing up. His speed and skill in high school earned him a scholarship to Florida State University. He was on the football, baseball, and track teams.

Sanders (right) tackles an opponent during a 1988 game with Florida State University.

Sanders (left) is chased by an opponent during a college game in 1986.

At Florida State, Sanders won two different titles for baseball and track in the same day. He began on the field with a baseball game in the afternoon. Then Sanders arrived at the track for an evening race. His team won the 4x100 meter relay. Fifteen minutes later, he was back at the baseball field. He then batted in two runs to help his team win and earn his second title that day.

Sanders played multiple sports in his pro career. In 1988, he was drafted by the New York Yankees in Major League Baseball. The next year, he was picked fifth overall by the Atlanta Falcons in the NFL Draft. The one-year contract Sanders signed with the Falcons made him the highest-paid cornerback in history.

Sanders, playing for the Atlanta Falcons, runs with the ball during a 1989 game.

CHAPTER 2

Gardner on defense in 2022

GOING PRO

Before Gardner joined the Jets in 2022, the team had one of the worst records in the league with only four wins. The year before, they only had two. But Gardner helped the Jets turn things around.

By Week 5 of the 2022 season, the Jets had a 2–2 record. On October 9, 2022, over 82,000 fans packed the Jets home stadium in New Jersey to watch them battle the Miami Dolphins. In the second quarter, the Dolphins quarterback ran for the end zone. Gardner tackled him before he could score.

The Jets soon took the lead. In the middle of the second quarter, they were up 12–7. The Dolphins quarterback made a throw. Gardner read the play perfectly. He sprinted down

Gardner tackles a Dolphins player on October 9, 2022.

the field. Then he leaped in front of the receiver to make the catch. That was Gardner's first NFL interception.

The Jets blew the game open after that. It ended in a 40–17 victory for the Jets. They won their next two games as well. But Gardner was just getting started.

In New York's Week 7 game against the Denver Broncos, Gardner put up his best numbers of the season. He had 10 tackles and three pass breakups. This earned him the Defensive Player of the Week award for the American Football Conference.

Gardner (right) defends against the Denver Broncos in 2022.

Sanders signed a contract with the San Francisco 49ers in 1994. That year, he had one of the best seasons of his career with six interceptions. He ran the interceptions back for a total of 303 yards and scored three touchdowns.

Sanders with the San Francisco 49ers in 1994

Sanders (left) on defense in 1994

Sanders and the 49ers won the National Football Conference that season. This earned them a spot in the Super Bowl. They faced the San Diego Chargers.

With about 13 minutes left on the game clock, the 49ers were up 49–18 against the Chargers. Desperate to stop the blowout, the Chargers made 13 plays in a row. They moved the ball 55 yards down the field. A touchdown was only one play away.

CONSIDER THIS

Sanders is a celebrity on and off the field. He has appeared in multiple TV ads and starred in a reality TV show with his family. Sauce Gardner is using his fame to explore his interests. He helped create a barbecue sauce called Sauce Sauce.

Sanders wasn't going to make it easy. He intercepted a pass from the Chargers quarterback. The 49ers won!

Sanders covers an opponent during the 1995 Super Bowl.

CHAPTER 3

Sanders plays for the Dallas Cowboys in 1997.

BUILDING A CHAMPION

Sanders was the top defensive player of every team he joined. His fame soared when he signed with the Dallas Cowboys in 1995. They won the National Football Conference. That made Sanders one of the few players to compete in back-to-back Super Bowls with different teams.

In the first quarter of the 1996 Super Bowl, Sanders caught a 47-yard pass from Cowboys quarterback Troy Aikman. The catch set up Dallas's first touchdown. It gave Sanders another first as well. He is the only NFL player to record both a catch and an interception in the Super Bowl. The game ended in a 27–17 victory over the Pittsburgh Steelers.

Sanders played four more seasons before joining the Washington Redskins in 2000. After one season with the team, Sanders retired. But he only stayed off the field for three years. He returned to play two seasons with the Baltimore Ravens before leaving the NFL for good in 2006.

Sanders (right) catches the ball during a 1996 Cowboys game.

CONSIDER THIS

Deion Sanders helped start the Prime Time Association. This group gives kids access to school and sports programs. Sauce Gardner helps young players succeed at football camps in Detroit.

From 1991 to 2006, Sanders was a first-team All-Pro six times. He played in eight Pro Bowl games. Sanders was only named NFL Defensive Player of the Year once, in 1994.

Sanders (left) attempts a tackle in the 1992 Pro Bowl.

Gardner accepts his Defensive Rookie of the Year award in 2022.

However, many fans think he's the best cornerback in NFL history.

Gardner hasn't been in the league for long. Even so, he's already made a name for himself. He won Defensive Rookie of the Year in 2022. He was also selected as a first-team All-Pro cornerback as a rookie. That hadn't happened in over 40 years!

As of 2023, the New York Jets hadn't had a winning season in 13 years. But Gardner is helping them rebuild. Many people think he's the player that will eventually lead them to another championship.

CHAPTER 4

Sanders speaks at the Pro Football Hall of Fame in 2011.

AND THE WINNER IS

In 2011, Deion Sanders strutted onto a football field in Canton, Ohio. He wasn't dressed to play. Instead, Prime Time wore golden shoes and a matching jacket. A crowd of 13,300 watched as he joined the Pro Football Hall of Fame.

It was a prime moment for Prime Time. He gave an emotional 10-minute speech thanking many people. He inspired even more.

Sauce Gardner was 11 years old when Sanders joined the Hall of Fame. In 2023, members of the media named Gardner as the league's best cornerback. They said he has a chance to match Sanders's career success.

In his first two NFL seasons, Gardner had two interceptions and 92 tackles. Sanders played 14 total seasons in the NFL. He made 53 interceptions and 254 tackles.

Gardner prepares to defend in 2023.

Gardner tracks the ball in a 2023 game.

Gardner has a long way to go, but that doesn't mean he can't win the smackdown. Sanders is still active in college football. Known as Coach Prime, he is the head coach of the University of Colorado Boulder football team. In 2023, he won the *Sports Illustrated* Sportsperson of the Year award for his work in Colorado.

Sanders and Gardner have both been the star of every team they've joined. It's okay for sports fans to compare athletes and have different opinions on who is better. Deion Sanders wins this smackdown for his impressive stats and skills. Who do you think is the winner? It's up to you to decide!

Sanders, playing for the Dallas Cowboys, runs with the ball during a 1996 game.

SMACKDOWN BREAKDOWN

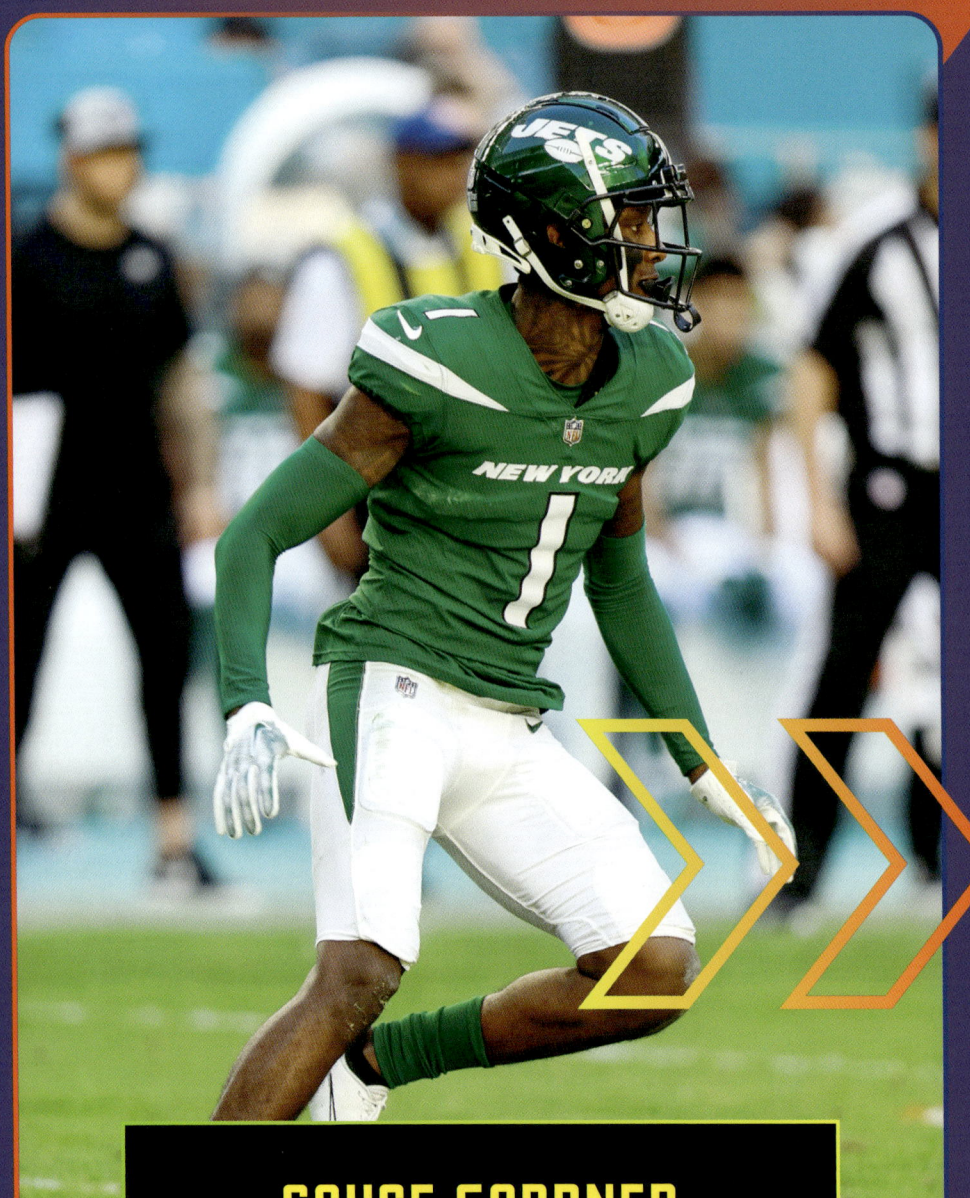

SAUCE GARDNER

Date of birth: August 31, 2000
Height: 6 feet 3 (1.9 m)
Pro Bowls: 2
First-Team All-Pros: 2

Stats are accurate through the 2023 NFL season.

DEION SANDERS

Date of birth: August 9, 1967
Height: 6 feet 1 (1.9 m)
Pro Bowls: 8
First-Team All-Pros: 6

GLOSSARY

cornerback: a defensive player that covers opposing receivers and tries to prevent passes to them

draft: when teams take turns choosing new players

end zone: the area at each end of a football field where players score touchdowns

first-team All-Pro: a team made up of each season's best NFL players

interception: a pass caught by the defending team

pro: short for *professional*, taking part in an activity to make money

Pro Bowl: the NFL's all-star game

punt: when a player drops the ball and kicks it before it touches the ground

rookie: a first-year player

scholarship: money that a school or another group gives to students to help pay for their education

title: a championship

wide receiver: a player whose main job is to catch passes

LEARN MORE

Britannica Kids: New York Jets
https://kids.britannica.com/students/article/New-York-Jets/571019

Coleman, Ted. *San Francisco 49ers*. Mendota Heights, MN: Press Room Editions, 2022.

Gigliotti, Jim. *The Story of the New York Jets*. Minneapolis: Kaleidoscope, 2020.

Kiddle: Deion Sanders
https://kids.kiddle.co/Deion_Sanders

Scheff, Matt. *The Super Bowl: Football's Game of the Year*. Minneapolis: Lerner Publications, 2021.

Sports Illustrated Kids: Football
https://www.sikids.com/football

INDEX

All-Pro, 4, 22–23
Atlanta Falcons, 13

cornerback, 4, 6, 8, 13, 23, 25

Dallas Cowboys, 20

Florida State University, 11–12

New York Jets, 4–5, 9, 14–16, 23

Pro Bowl, 4, 22
Pro Football Hall of Fame, 24–25

San Francisco 49ers, 17–19
Super Bowl, 4, 18, 20–21

University of Cincinnati, 8–9

PHOTO ACKNOWLEDGMENTS

Image credits: AP Photo/Tom DiPace, pp. 4, 26, 28; AP Photo/Peter Read Miller, pp. 5, 7, 13, 20, 29; AP Photo/Lauren Bacho, p. 6; Joe Robbins/Icon Sportswire/Getty Images, p. 8; Kevin Schultz/CSM/Alamy, p. 9; AP Photo/Michael Allio/Icon Sportswire, p. 10; Rich Clarkson/Sports Illustrated/Getty Images, p. 11; John Biever/Sports Illustrated/Getty Images, p. 12; AP Photo/Rich Graessle/Icon Sportswire, p. 14; AP Photo/Duncan Williams/CSM, p. 15; AP Photo/Michael Owens, p. 16; Focus on Sport/Getty Images, p. 17; Mickey Pfleger/Sports Illustrated/Getty Images, p. 18; Joseph Patronite/Getty Images, p. 19; Richard Mackson/Sports Illustrated/Getty Images, p. 21; AP Photo/Paul Spinelli, p. 22; AP Photo/David J. Phillip, p. 23; Frank Jansky/Southcreek Global/Alamy, p. 24; AP Photo/Cooper Neill, p. 25; AP Photo/Greg Trott, p. 27.

Cover: AP Photo/Paul Spinelli; AP Photo/Scott Boehm.